DATE DUE

			PRINTED IN U.S.A.

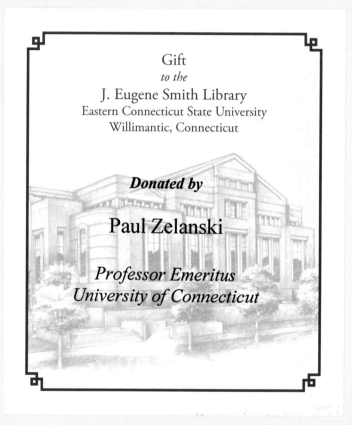

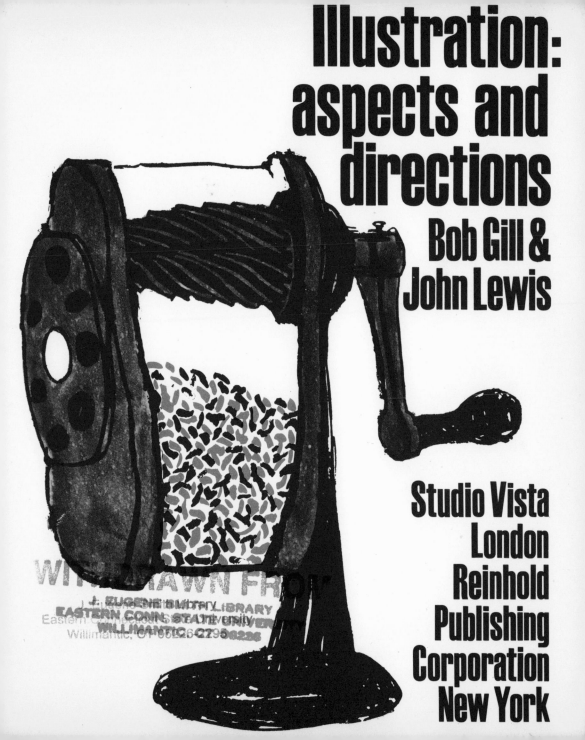

Illustration: aspects and directions

Bob Gill & John Lewis

Studio Vista
London
Reinhold
Publishing
Corporation
New York

PUBLISHED IN LONDON BY STUDIO VISTA LTD
BLUE STAR HOUSE, HIGHGATE HILL, N19
AND IN NEW YORK, 1964
BY REINHOLD PUBLISHING CORPORATION,
430 PARK AVENUE, NEW YORK
REPRINTED 1965
LIBRARY OF CONGRESS CATALOG NUMBER 64 - 17538
PRINTED IN THE NETHERLANDS
BY N.V. DRUKKERIJ KOCH & KNUTTEL, GOUDA

Contents

The purpose of this book is to put into perspective what we think about certain aspects of illustration. Illustration is a lot of things. It can be considered as a work of art or as a visual answer to a specific literary problem. Or it can be both. It can provide information, or elucidation. It can be a means of social comment or it can entertain.

Most of the examples that we show here are by contemporary American and British artists who use illustration as a means of personal expression. These drawings speak for themselves, they need no comment from us. We have chosen them because they illustrated our theme better than any others we could find, not because they were necessarily better (or worse) than all the others we would have liked to have included..

We have limited our text to a series of short introductions to each chapter. When we have referred to certain artists and art movements it is to help establish influences and trends that appear in contemporary work.

London 1964

J. Thompson, Adolphe Smith
Photograph of Recruiting Sergeants, 1876

Fox Talbot, on the day in 1841, when he patented his process for successfully fixing photographic prints, also drove the first nail into the coffin of the recording illustrator. Things and people would never look the same again. Academic conventions that had governed both painting and illustration were soon to be thrown overboard. Within a few years the camera was doing the job of the recording illustrator, and more authoritatively. Artists working for the *Graphic* or *Illustrated London News*, such as H. C. Seppings Wright, Melton Prior, or Craig and Hatherell who combined so successfully in working on the same drawings of scenes of disaster, war or pomp and ceremony (we believe Craig did the left side of the drawing and Hatherell the right), were replaced by anonymous journalist-cameramen, who in their turn produced *artists* in their own medium (such as Gene Smith or H. Cartier-Bresson).

The belief that Art was a matter of faithful recording in tone and colour of the surface appearance of things was a particularly nineteenth-century phenomenon. When the French Impressionist painters such as Monet, Seurat or Degas really recorded the visual appearance of things in terms of light (using a divided palette of the spectrum) and the haphazard arrangements that objects and people occupy so naturally, their work was not understood. Yet what they did was (accepting the limitations of hand and brush and paint) just what the colour camera does today even more efficiently. In our age, accustomed to seeing things in terms of colour photography, technicolour movies and so on, it is

G. Durand
Zulu War 1879 Wood engraving from *The Graphic*

no wonder that the Impressionists have achieved such a fantastic popularity and that their work should be so eagerly sought by the rich men and museum directors of the Western world.

Art directors and others who commission illustrations now have a decision to make. Either they use photographers, or artists. For most kinds of reportage, the camera provides the quickest and usually the most successful answer. If an illustrator is asked to do such work, he must provide something more. Apart from the economic advantages (especially for letterpress printing) in the reproduction of his line drawings, there is the incalculable value of the personality of line itself.

There is little room for the illustrator who wishes to draw life-like representations of the finish of the Kentucky Derby, or any other news story that needs pictorial reporting. The camera can do it all. On the other hand, a sensitive draughtsman may be able to make more pointed, more formidable social comment than the camera can ever do. Daumier's judges and lawyers, Max Beerbohm's Pre-Raphaelites, Toulouse-Lautrec's harlots, are all fairly obvious examples of this. Less obvious are those highly skilful, usually anonymous 'breakdown' drawings of motorcar engines and other pieces of machinery, which not even an X-ray camera could do so efficiently.

The camera and the pen line can both form a valid vocabulary for the illustrator. If he is an artist, it will show in his work, whatever the medium.

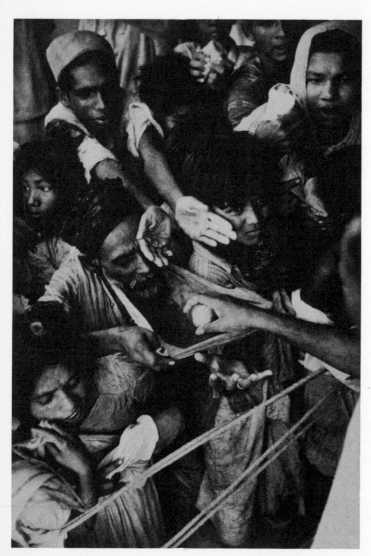

Henri Cartier-Bresson
The Decisive Moment

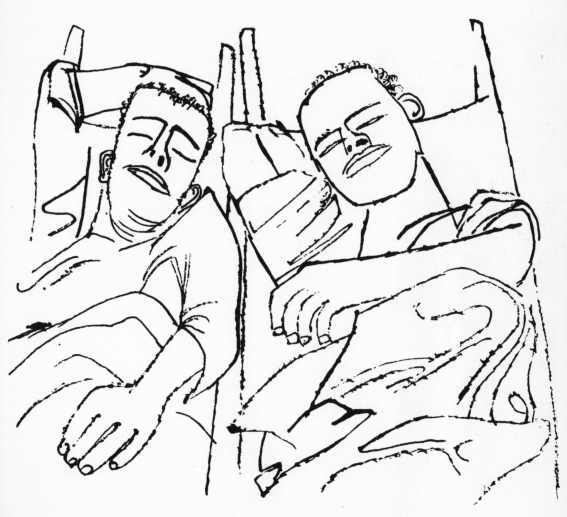

Ben Shahn
The Untouchables

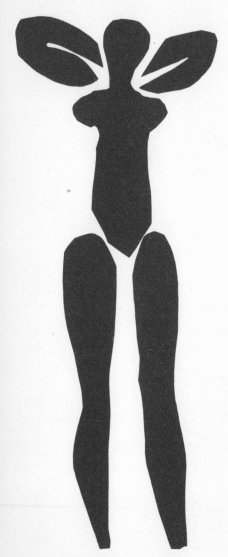

Henri Matisse
'La Perruche et la Sirène'

A question that is often asked is, 'Is illustration art?' Of course it is, if the illustrator is an artist. Painters and sculptors such as Chagall and Henry Moore have brought new life to book illustration, but this is only one very small aspect of illustration. A random list of the various kinds of illustration might range from comic strips to those for limited editions. An illustrator should still be able to do good work, even in the least esoteric of these fields. He may well ask what is good illustration and what is bad, and why?

And when we say bad, we do not necessarily mean bad art, but bad illustration. By illustration we mean any form of exposition or elucidation. The degree it elucidates or reveals is the degree of its goodness or badness. It can exist on its own, or it may need to be amplified by words. Or it can itself amplify a text. It can also serve decorative ends. It can be a drawing, a painting, a collage or a photograph; it can also be a thumb-print, a geometrical diagram, an ink blot or anything else that communicates. It should always be judged by the effectiveness of its statement and the media in which it appears. Brashness, even vulgarity, may have a place, just as much as subtlety and sophistication.

Illustration as a facet of graphic *art* is judged on the level of any other means of artistic expression. Illustration as an element in graphic *design* must be judged primarily on its success or failure to make its point. Frequently it is judged on both levels.

Artist unknown
Magazine cover

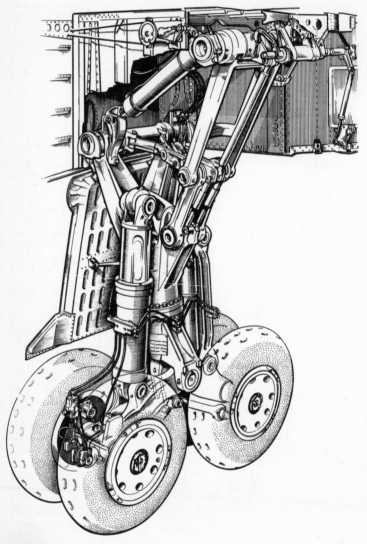

C. V. Misstear
Cut-away drawing, aircraft undercarriage

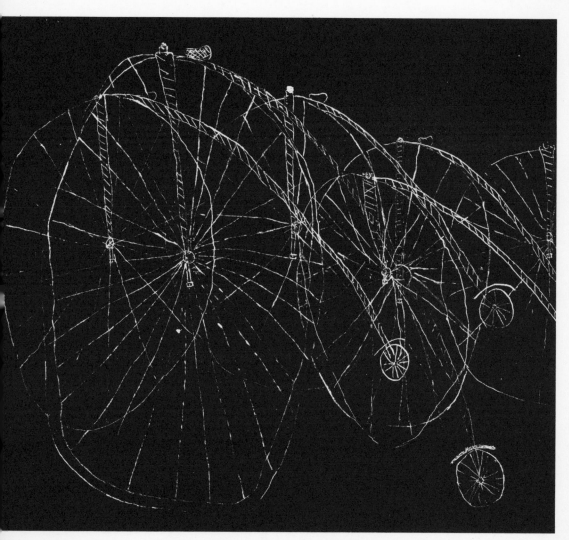

hild's drawing
'enny Farthing Bikes'

Alain F. LeFoll
Political cartoon

Ronald Shakespeare
Collage

Tomi Ungerer
WHK Radio advertisement

Pierre Bonnard
'Sainte Monique'

Thomas Bewick
Tail pieces to *A History of British Birds*, 1797

Every good illustration must have something to say. The illustrator must commit himself. He should not need to rely on lengthy captions. From Thomas Bewick's time onwards one can trace a line of commentator-illustrators who have influenced the work of their modern counterparts. If one looks outside the pages of books and periodicals, one could go back to long before Bewick, to Carpaccio's scenes of Venice in the fifteenth century or to Brueghel's fear-stricken Flemish peasants, or to Hogarth's boozy, lusty, gambling England of the mid-eighteenth century, or to Goya's blood-chilling horrors of war.

We think it is worth devoting some space to a few of these commentator-illustrators who have in one way or another influenced modern illustration. Our somewhat arbitrary choice has led us to look at Bewick, Rowlandson, Daumier, Lautrec and Max Beerbohm. All members of this oddly assorted quintet have this in common, that each had an utterly personal comment to make.

Bewick's claim to fame has rested largely on the fact that he rescued wood engraving from oblivion, and that by his superb skill in this medium produced illustrations with much of the delicacy of steel or copper intaglio engraving, but which could be printed at the same time as the letterpress. Much has been made of his use of the white line, regarded by his historians as a remarkable invention. In fact, Bewick was trained as an intaglio engraver on metal and used exactly the same technique for engraving on the end grain of boxwood. So his intaglio lines

Thomas Rowlandson
'Dressing for the Masquerade' 1788

Honoré Daumier
Lithograph for *Le Charivari,* 1851

printed black from the wiped metal plate and white from the inked wood.

We suggest that Bewick's importance as an illustrator was not so much for his precise delineation of birds and beasts in his *Aesop's Fables, Quadrupeds* and *History of British Birds,* but for the shrewd comment with which he revealed in the very small compass of a tail-piece the daily life of the Northumbrian countryside, without any resource to caption or literary content. These little cuts give one a very clear idea of life in the border country, particularly outdoor life, a century and a half ago. The callous cruelty of the age is shown here in the illustration of the children on the village green chasing a dog with a can tied to its tail, whilst an aproned man, perhaps their father, looks approvingly on. Humour runs through many of these engravings, such as one of a drunken man staggering home under two crescent moons. But the most common theme, most tellingly revealed, is the weather. Bewick was, of course, a countryman, but so perhaps to a lesser extent were his pupils, who did many of the tail-pieces for these books. The cuts of the fisherman sheltering behind a tree in driving rain and the cormorant standing alone on its tide-washed rock facing the wintry wastes of the North Sea are enough to send shivers down one's back. This is true comment.

It would be difficult to think of two illustrators less alike in background or tastes than Thomas Bewick and his contemporary Thomas Rowlandson. Rowlandson was a sophisticated man-about-town, completely bilingual, as much at home in

H. de Toulouse-Lautrec
Poster for May Belfort

Paris as he was in London. Bewick, after one short visit to London, never went near the place again.

Rowlandson, one of the finest draughtsmen this country has ever produced, used his incomparable curving line to record for posterity the follies and the comedies of the last years of England before the Industrial Revolution laid so much of it waste. His work was divided between water colour painting, book illustration and cartoons. In the latter he was to some extent influenced by his friend James Gillray, a greater cartoonist if a lesser artist.

Rowlandson was befriended by a German called Rudolph Ackerman, who provided him with a certain and substantial income, in return for a wide range of prints and drawings, including the adventures of a peripatetic parson called Dr Syntax. The Ackerman prints were etched by Rowlandson, usually aquatinted by a professional engraver and then, following a master copy, were skilfully coloured by Ackerman's own artists. These delicately coloured prints are very different from the coarse, garish prints produced by Rowlandson's other publishers, who were obviously working for a different market. Talking about his printmaking, Rowlandson once remarked that he reckoned he had engraved enough copper to sheathe a first-rate man-of-war.

When Rowlandson died in 1827, one year before Bewick, the greatest of the European commentator-illustrators of the age was only nineteen. This was the French lithographer and painter, Honoré Daumier, who followed a Hogarthian line of illustrating the lives of the *petits bourgeois*, who were then feeling

Max Beerbohm
Portrait of Oscar Wilde

the dire after-effects of the French Revolution. Daumier's output of lithographs, particularly for the daily paper *Le Charivari*, was phenomenal. His drawings are often vulgar, slick, even repellant. But like Rowlandson before him, on occasions he reached sublime heights of draughtsmanship. As a caricaturist he has never been equalled.

Henri de Toulouse-Lautrec and Max Beerbohm were artists of different generations, tastes and talents, but both were astringent commentators. Lautrec's drawings and lithographs of the gas-lit music halls, circuses and stews of Montmartre today rest in the unlikely setting of the Bishop's Palace at Albi. These brilliant drawings were the forerunners of his theatrical posters, which were influenced by Japanese prints and were masterly pieces of illustration.

Max Beerbohm poked quiet ridicule at both his contemporaries and at the figures of the recent past. These ranged from the reigning Monarch to the Pre-Raphaelite painters. The physical likenesses of Swinburne and Rossetti are fixed for ever by Beerbohm's drawings in *Rossetti and his Circle*, where they are gently satirized. The drawing here of Oscar Wilde is not so gentle. The human scene must always attract the attention of artists with a feeling for the frailties and follies of their fellow men. Different ages will of course produce different graphic responses.

George Grosz
'The Parasites'

Gerard Hoffnung
The Hoffnung Symphony Orchestra

R. O. Blechman
Punch

Oskar Kokoschka
Christmas Poster

Kaethe Kollwitz
Poster

Tomi Ungerer
Esquire magazine

José Luis Cuevas
'Kafka'

Felix Topolski
Topolski's Chronicle

Robert Weaver
Portraits of Washington and Leonard Bernstein. *Show* magazine

Charles Dana Gibson
Our Neighbours, 1910

Illustration has become a somewhat derogatory term. It is comparable to the word 'literary', which has often been used in a disparaging way about the paintings that used to appear in the Royal Academy or the Salon, with such titles as 'A glass of wine with Caesar Borgia' or 'When did you last see your father?'. The essence of these paintings was the literary content rather than the aesthetic. After a long period of revulsion against such banal work, and an insistence on the qualities of form and colour and, finally, of abstraction, there is already a tentative return to the associated ideas of literary art. This can be seen in the work of certain painters such as Francis Bacon, or in the 'Pop artists' of America or Britain.

Illustration has laboured under the handicap of being considered a separate activity, beneath the notice of 'serious' painters. The productions of Ambroise Vollard, whose magnificent folios were 'illustrated' by artists such as Picasso, Rouault, Derain, etc, did little to change this attitude, for these books were only an excuse for graphically-minded artists to exercise their talents on the lithographic stone or etching plate.

Slowly the attitude has changed. In 1906, to compare the work of an *avant garde* painter, such as Picasso, with a leading illustrator such as Charles Dana Gibson, produces a laughable comparison (to us in the 1960s; in 1906 the laugh, except for the very, very few, would have been in the other direction).

Today there should be no difference in the aesthetic standards of painting and illustration. After a long

34

Pablo Picasso
Woodcut, 1906

period of stagnation it is coming into its own again.
It is a pity that so few good painters are being com-
missioned or are unwilling to work in this field
of illustration.

One of the early influences in this return to an
acceptance of literary values in art is Dada. The
Dadaists consciously rejected conventional methods
of painting and made use of graphics as an 'uoconta-
minated' medium. They made use of typographic
symbols and also of illustration. For this, as well as
producing rather crude woodcuts they assembled
old engravings from catalogues of furniture or hard-
ware or from typefounders' specimen books. The
most odd juxtaposition of cut-throat razors, camels,
balloons and pissoirs, or of ornamental porcelain
stoves, cane furniture, pantechnicons and pumps
produced a startling, even shocking effect on whatever audience they were aiming at – and that could
only be one – for their object was *épater la bourgeoisie*.
The main vehicle for Dada expression was literature.
Illustration rather than painting is the natural bed-
fellow for literature. As they withdrew into the
world of childhood – the name Dada is one of the
first childish sounds – so they could make use for
their illustrations of a kind of children's first-primer-
in-reading illustration technique. Though the Dadaists intended to jolt the complacency out of a world
that could stomach the charnel-house atmosphere
of Ypres and Passchendaele, they spoke to too small
an audience; yet like a pebble chucked into a mill-
pool the ripples have reached this generation, nearly
half a century later.

The Hon. John Collier
'A glass of wine with Caesar Borgia'

If the Dadaists had done nothing else, they would be remembered for smashing the conventions of graphic communication. Without Dada, there would have been no 'Pop Art'. Dada illustration was motivated by literary intent. This puts all its emphasis on the component parts of an illustration or pasted-up collage and little on its skill in execution. 'Pop Art' picks up some elements of Dada, treating art as being as consumable as an iced lolly, or as expendable as a bus ticket. The 'Pop Artist' fills his pictures with the little things of our urban life, such as pin-ups, matchbox covers, cigarette packs and badges, to indicate status, whether it is for Wolf Cubs and Brownies or a Junior Movie Club. This is illustration, understandable and experienced by a public conditioned by the mass-market techniques of advertising and T.V. It is a public living 'in a world of cafés and Coke culture'* with standards based on an acceptance of present day built-in obsolescence. That much of what the Pop artist paints looks pretty tawdry is only a reflection of the world he lives in. He prefers to accept it rather than to retreat into a world of negation like the Dadaists or into a world of make-believe. The majority of the contemporary illustrations in this book, though in no way pieces of Pop art, are drawn by artists who have accepted, however reluctantly, their twentieth-century environment.

* David Sylvester: *Sunday Times* London 26 Jan. 1964.

Paul Davis
Push Pin Graphic

David Hockney
Etching for *A Rake's Progress*

Peter Blake
Town magazine

Seymour Chwaste, Allen Vogel
'Diary of a Madman' *Push Pin Graphic*

Gunther Kieser
'Die Schreckenskammer', _Kriminal Sonette_ by Ludwig Rubiner

Barbara Nessim
'Coney Island' *Gentlemen* magazine

Patrick Hughes
Painting

George Hoy
Cartoon

A drawing of a face need not be a map of a face, not even a contour map. The line, by its quality, or the space encompassed by that line can suggest far more than any painstaking 'map'. In this way, the artist reveals the characterization, or the humour, or the pathos of a subject. The wit or the sadness lies in the line itself. An artist like Tenniel, beloved though his *Alice in Wonderland* drawings have been for several generations, could no more draw a witty line than fly, whereas every pencil mark by Ronald Searle shows something of his humour. The expressive line runs through all good illustration. In an age of hurry, the economy of a linear statement has an immediate appeal. Primitive man first expressed himself on cave walls by line. The fabulous drawings of animals at Lascaux in the Dordogne are essentially line illustration. Primitive races today, when first confronted with photographs, cannot read them, for they are searching for linear expression. Tone and chiaroscuro mean nothing to them. Illustration by line was one of the first methods of visual communication, and it still works today.

Illustration now occupies a very different place from the one it had in the nineteenth century. The great illustrators of that time worked for the publishers of the three-decker novels; the names of Cruikshank, Phiz, Leach, du Maurier and Millais were as familiar as the names of comic strip characters, if not the names of their creators, are today. Their drawings or engravings recorded scenes and events already described in loving detail by their authors. Cruikshank and Phiz (H. K. Browne) with

R. R. Bouché
CBS Radio advertisement

Dickens, Leach with Surtees, Millais with Trollope and of course Tenniel with Lewis Carroll. The work of the same artists certainly appeared in magazines such as *Punch*, though some, such as that fine draughtsman Charles Keene, rarely strayed into book pages, but confined themselves to social comment in the periodicals.

No publisher today would dream of launching a new novel with illustrations. One of the last 'important' pieces of book illustration in England was *The Forsyte Saga*, illustrated by Anthony Gross in 1951. Though this book had never been out of print in thirty years, the Gross edition subsequently sold over 50,000 copies. There were many reasons for this. The most powerful of them was that here was a twentieth-century artist of stature, who had worked in various fields of communication, including cartoon films such as his *Joie de Vivre* and *The Fox Hunt*. He was able to add a new dimension to Galsworthy's prose, for it to be read again in mid-twentieth century terms. And here was a supreme example of the use of line, tentative, wavering or as bold as brass, weaving arabesques round Galsworthy's solid English characters, and revealing even more vividly than the author's pen the sense of style still possessed by that particular strata of English society.

These drawings by Anthony Gross show much that we have been trying to say about line. His use of impressed patterns of lace to give a richness to a woman's dress, his contrast of heavy brush strokes and the most tentative of pen lines are not stylistic

Anthony Gross
The Forsyte Saga

tricks, but relate directly to content.

Ronald Searle's nervous spiky line is no mannerist trick. It is the natural means of expression of an urgently sensitive draughtsman.

Ben Shahn's barbed wire line encompasses more than a barbed wit. His paintings have often been concerned with themes possessing some social implication, such as the Sacco-Vanzetti case. He is a story-teller; his interests are profound, social and humanitarian. His training was varied, but included working for some years as a lithographer's apprentice. His work is very human. He sets his figures in deeply understood architectural settings. The drawings for the film *Ambassador Satchmo* in 1956 show these settings of frame houses and New England churches superbly well.

Shahn's drawings of pieces of machinery, such as aged typewriters, or agricultural implements, or pieces of furniture, are all imbued with a life of their own. An illustration of empty chairs and empty music stands, all obviously waiting for their musicians to return, shows this quality. Shahn has always been interested in typography. The way he handles lettering such as in a street scene with signs like 'Olden Drugs', 'Soda', 'Coca-cola', etc, makes one look again at this kind of alphabetical clutter in the main drag of any home town. Ben Shahn is essentially an illustrator. He brings lustre to the profession.

André François
The Half Naked Knight

Ben Shahn
Book jacket, *Ounce Dice Trice*

Ronald Searle
Which way did he go?

Jack Wolfgang Beck
Booklet, School of Visual Arts

Thomas Allen
Booklet, School of Visual Arts

Milton Glaser
Push Pin Graphic

Henri Matisse
'Les Fleurs du Mal'

Aztec stamp
Chalco, Mexico

Milton Glaser
Life magazine advertisement

Emmy Andriesse
Photograph of the ruined castle at Montmajour.
The World of Van Gogh, 1953

Style is the quality in an artist's work that comes from something within the man. It is a result of an artist seeing something in a special, private way. He then transmits that personal vision in his own idiosyncratic manner. It is quite futile for a student to try to imitate an artist's style, for it means he is trying to see with another man's eyes.

Style is not the same thing as method. The way an artist composes his scenes, fixes his poses, or makes use of palpable clichés is all part of his method of working. This is open to any would-be illustrator to admire and emulate. It is only natural for the student, in his search for expression, to imitate the work of the artists he admires. More often than not, he will be influenced by the work of another student, who no doubt in his turn has taken the trouble to find out how some artist he likes really has drawn an eye, an arm, a figure or a tree.

This is not altogether bad, as it provides him with some means, however artificial, for expressing himself, but it is only a stage in his development. Unless his style ultimately reflects his personal vision, he has little to offer as an artist. The way he expresses himself *must* be his own.

Vincent van Gogh
Drawing of the castle at Montmajour

Robert Weaver
Portraits of Rockefeller and Nixon, *Esquire* magazine

Harvey Schmidt
Portrait of McCarthy, *Esquire* magazine

Oskar Kokoschka
Self-portrait

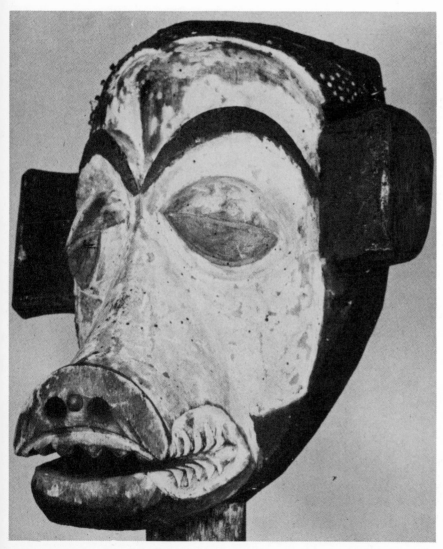

Mask
Belgian Congo

Carol Annand
Queen magazine

R. O. Blechman
Esquire magazine

Edvard Munch
'The Room of the Dead'

Seymour Chwaste
Push Pin Graphic

Paul Klee
'Air-tsu-dni

Child's drawing
'Crocodile'

Isadore Seltzer
Push Pin Graphic

Jerome Snyder
CBS Radio advertisement

Pierre Bonnard
Sheet music cover

Phil Hayes
School of Visual Arts magazine

George Cruikshank
Oliver Twist, 1838

George Cruikshank was a contemporary of Daumier. As a commentator, he lacked the great French lithographer's biting wit. His output of work was at least as great as Daumier's, but most of it was for the illustration of works of fiction. Daumier and Cruikshank had one thing in common at least, and that was their attitude to drawing from models: 'One denied that he ever drew from life and the other was never seen to do so.' *

Cruikshank will probably be remembered more for his drawings for *Oliver Twist* than for anything else. The picture of 'Fagin in the Condemned Cell' must be one of the most famous illustrations of any time. Yet everything about it is a cliché; the characterization, the pose, the treatment of the staring eyes and the lighting. The clichés of types, poses and situations that Cruikshank used would all be familiar to the readers of the novels that he illustrated – so that without any painful mental gymnastics they could accept the scene before them. These exaggerations would be even more familiar to theatre-goers of a later generation who had seen Henry Irving playing Shylock at the Lyceum.

The secret of the success of an artist like Cruikshank or, indeed, Rowlandson, is that they produce the illusion of life, almost in the way that a stage producer might. Their stock figures are like little puppets that are set on a stage that we view, as if we were on the other side of the proscenium arch. These puppets have life breathed into them, by

* Edward Ardizzone *The Born Illustrator*. Motif 1

72

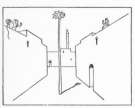
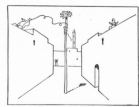
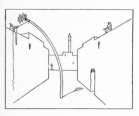
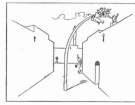
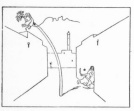
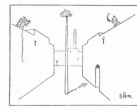

Caran d'Ache
'Oriental Romance' *c* 1890

their creators' constant return to nature.

Though the 'Condemned Cell' may be the most famous illustration of Fagin, the one we show here, 'Oliver introduced to the Respectable Old Gentleman', is more typical and less melodramatic. There is much acute observation in the setting, including 'The last dying speech' broadsheet pinned up above the fireplace. The characterizations of Fagin and the Artful Dodger are established for all time in this drawing; the 'young gentlemen' sucking their churchwarden pipes might have been drawn by the *Daily Express* cartoonist Giles; only Oliver does not ring true, but that was as much the author's fault as the illustrator's.

The Victorian age was the age of reading, and the age of the serial. The soap opera of today is only the degenerate offspring of this hardy perennial. However worried we get over the vicissitudes of 'Lil' Abner' or 'the Archers', it is hard to realize that half the English-speaking world went into mourning when the number of *The Old Curiosity Shop* came out with the death of 'Little Nell' (one of Dickens's most long-suffering characters).

All these serials were fully illustrated, presenting the illustrators as much as the authors with a pretty severe test of consistency. Yet how well such artists as Hablot K. Browne and Marcus Stone met these periodical demands.

Just as much consistency is demanded today by the readers of the 'comics', whether they are faithfully following the fortunes of their space travellers, lovelorn heroines or other characters, human and

" There will be nineteen extra to lunch to-day."

Pont (Graham Laidler)
Punch c 1940

animal, anthropomorphic or otherwise. We do not know who was the first comic-strip artist. The first master of the medium was Emmanuel Poiré, who was born in 1858 and died in 1909. He drew under the pseudonym of Caran d'Ache (which means lead pencil). Whilst most of his contemporaries produced joke drawings that needed twenty-five-line captions, Caran d'Ache limited himself to a brief title and then told his story without words. His work was in the tradition of French caricature, at that time the best in the world. His drawing was economical and extremely pointed. It does not look dated today, yet humour can date more than anything, for instance the limericks of Edward Lear (1812–1888), may seem to belong to a bygone age, but not his droll drawings. His illustrations have a kind of nervous urgency about them, as if the poor little man had been trying to complete them before being over-taken by his next epileptic fit. They are also, in the most uncompromising way, very decorative. A twen-tieth-century artist, whose early work had a close affinity to Lear's, is Edward Bawden. Bawden is also possessed of a most quirky sense of humour, which was brilliantly revealed in his drawings for Shell-on-the-Road press advertisements in the 1930s. This humour runs through all his work, hand in hand with an even greater decorative sense than Lear possessed. Graham Laidler (Pont) drew in *Punch* in the 1930s and late '40s. Under the generic title of 'The British Character', his drawings reflected most brilliantly the end of a social period.

I've forgotten what
I came here to
talk about

John Glashan
The Eye of the Needle

Edward Lear
A Book of Nonsense, 1861

Edward Bawden
Shell-Mex advertisement c 1930

Milton Caniff
Comic strip

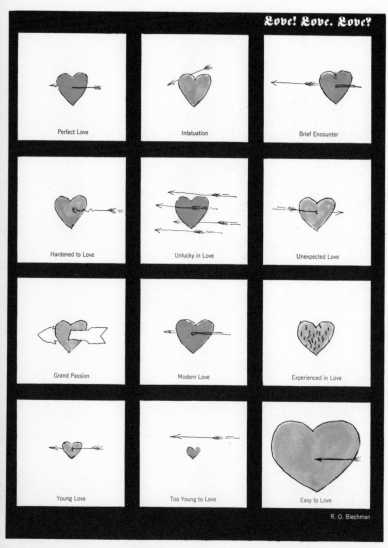

R. O. Blechman
Esquire magazine

Raoul Dufy
'La terre frottée d'ail'

Lou Meyers
New York Times advertisement

Simon was sent to market,
To buy a joint of meat,
He tied it to his horse's tail,
To keep it clean and sweet.

He went to slide upon the ice,
Before the ice would bear,
Then he plunged in above his knees,
Which made poor Simon stare.

He went to shoot a wild duck,
But the duck flew away,
Says Simon I can't hit him,
Because he would not stay.

Then Simple Simon went a hunting,
For to catch a hare,
He rode an ass about the street,
But could not find one there.

J. Catnach
Chapbook woodcuts c 1800

He went for water in a seive,
But soon it all run through,
And went all o'er his clothes,
Which made poor Simon rue.

He washed himself with blacking
ball,
Because he had no soap,
And then said to his mother
I'm a beauty now I hope.

He went to eat some honey,
Out of the mustard pot,
It bit his tongue until he cried,
That was all the good he got.

Simple Simon cutting his mother's
bellows open to see where the wind
lay.

Amongst children's books, the simplicity, vitality, even crudity, of the cuts in the eighteenth- and early nineteenth-century chapbooks are very hard to match. These were produced by anonymous artists for little print shops in the cities of Britain and America. James Catnach of the Seven Dials Press published many of these little books, in between printing 'Last Dying Confessions' of the most recently convicted murderers. The chapbook technique was used by Dr Heinrich Hoffman for his *Struwwelpeter*, first published in Germany in 1845. The woodcut is, however, replaced by the lithographic stone and the drawings are about as unselfconsciously humorous as their woodcut predecessors.

Children's books have moved through various stages of sophistication, naïvety and sentimentality. The anthropomorphism of Puss-in-Boots was carried to charming heights by Beatrix Potter (1866–1943) with her water colour drawings for *The Tailor of Gloucester*, *Peter Rabbit*, etc. The followers of Walt Disney vulgarized this approach, but reached even wider markets. Jean de Brunhof's endearing picture stories of *Babar the Elephant* were an exception to this decline; they were in the tradition of Edy Legrand's *Macao et Cosmage*, colourful, gay and witty. One or two children's book illustrators have achieved even closer links with their authors than Phiz ever had with Dickens or John Leach with Surtees. Tenniel's *Alice* and A. B. Frost's *Uncle Remus* are perhaps the most obvious examples.

Tenniel is eternally linked to *Alice*; a rather unimaginative political cartoonist was here inspired by

Dr Heinrich Hoffmann
'The Story of Little Suck-a-thumb', lithograph
for *Struwwelpeter*, 1845

Lewis Carroll's nonsense, and actually aided by the author's sketches. The 'unimaginative political cartoonist' has joined the immortals – if illustrators can be allowed a modest immortality. It is difficult to pick out any of the illustrations – they are all good – and they are as much a part of one's mental picture of the book as are Lewis Carroll's words. The illustrator here is enlarging on the author's words and is really heightening the reader's pleasure. What better can he do than that?

Joel Chandler Harris wrote to A. B. Frost, the illustrator of *Uncle Remus* and said: 'You have made the book so much your own, you had better consider it yours.' Or words to that effect. Such a close identity of purpose, it must be admitted, is somewhat rare. Most of the really successful children's books have come from one hand, where the author has been his own illustrator or the illustrator his own author.

One of the first successful English artist-authors of illustrated children's books was Kate Greenaway. In 1878, Edmund Evans printed a first edition of 20,000 of her first book *Under the Window*. It sold out immediately and before long it had passed the 100,000 mark. These pretty delicate water-colours of children dressed in garments that no children had ever worn were printed from woodblocks engraved by Edmund Evans. The technique of reproducing these drawings is of some interest. Evans photographed the original water-colours on to the surface of a woodblock; engraved them, as nearly facsimile as possible, then transferred this impression on to

Sir John Tenniel
'Alice and the White Queen' wood engraving
for *Alice Through the Looking-Glass* 1887

other woodblocks to engrave the other colours.* Kate Greenaway's talent as an artist was apparently slight, yet her books have had a surprising durability and delighted many succeeding generations.

In 1919, a young French artist called Edy Legrand wrote and illustrated a colourful child's book about the South Seas called *Macao et Cosmage*. In a large square format, these illustrations were boldly drawn and lithographed in flat areas of colour, showing the influence of Raoul Dufy, yet personal to Legrand. This was the first of a number of gay, pretty books illustrated by Legrand. Ten years later Legrand illustrated in line with stencil colour two delightful little books, in landscape format, called *Bolivar* and *Lafayette*. Technically the most effective of Legrand's work (published by A. Tolmer) was *La Nuit de la St Sylvaine*, which he lithographed in the mid-thirties, but a certain sentimentality had by that time crept into his work. Largely through Legrand a new pattern had been established for children's books. Another French publisher, Flammarion, at this time produced a series of books for children in a landscape format. The most successful of these were drawn by a Russian, Rojankovsky, who used a simple, posterish technique for his colourful drawings of seals, squirrels and other animals.

In England, apart from a tentative effort made by the publisher Daniel O'Connor in 1921 who used the artist Claud Lovat Fraser, there was little sign of

* Percy H. Muir *Notes on the occasion of the centenary of K. G.* Alphabet and Image 1

A. B. Frost
Uncle Remus, 1880

change. Lovat Fraser, an artist with a finely developed decorative sense, illustrated *The Woodcutter's Dog* and *The Luck of the Beanrows*, both translated from the French of Charles Nodier; these little drawings were in the chapbook style. Though Lovat Fraser usually drew with a reed pen, these little decorations are in ordinary pen line with stencilled flat colours. It was not until Sir Allen Lane, of Penguin Books, launched his Puffin series of books during the Second World War, in a landscape format similar to Flammarion's books, that a fresh approach to children's books was made. These varied from books about war, aeroplanes, and butterflies to Kathleen Hale's *Orlando the Marmalade Cat* or to Edward Bawden's most decorative *The Arabs*.

One of the few exceptions to the general run of mediocrity in English and American children's books of the pre-war years was *Little Tim and the Brave Sea Captain*, written and illustrated by Edward Ardizzone, an English artist in the direct tradition of Cruikshank. Ardizzone's work is filled with a pre-first-war, almost Victorian atmosphere, yet his children's books, such as the *Little Tim* series, are uniquely popular on both sides of the Atlantic. He is a real illustrator, with the ability to set a scene with only the slightest resource to period props. The details of drawing-room, street scene, dock side or ship board are of the slightest, yet the atmosphere seems right. He has no compunction about using 'bubbles' when someone is talking, whether it is only a 'Bravo! Tim' or 'Armed with a rifle I kept the night watch'. Anything that will help his purpose of

putting over his illustrations and so establishing contact with his readers he rightly regards as justified.

Over the last few years new life has been injected into children's books. Artists and designers working in graphic design have become dissatisfied with the scope and excitement offered to them in these fields. Many of them solve their commercial problems with superb skill, yet still find themselves filled with an urge for self-expression. 'Sunday Painting' is no remedy for graphic designers, however appropriate it may be for truck drivers or bank managers. Books, their own books, however, are within their scope of verbal and visual communication. And of books, children's books offer the most direct and simple challenge. So these artist-designers have directed their sometimes considerable talents in this direction, usually acting both as author and illustrator. They tend to make their texts amplify their illustrations.

This impetus has been felt in art schools, and a number of young artists have produced children's books of originality and charm. This work of quality is still only a drop in the ocean of mediocrity. The fault lies squarely with the publishers and the booksellers who are, as ever, only too happy to have again what they had before.

Antonio Frasconi
See and Say

Joseph Low
Mother Goose Riddle Rhymes

A PEINE AVAIT IL ETREINT MACAO ET SALUE COS-MAGE, EMUE, QUE DEJA IL VOGUAIT VERS SON CROISEUR....

MACAO FUT TRISTE LONGTEMPS...CETTE VISITE L'AVAIT TRANSFORMÉ..SA SOLITUDE LUI PARAISSAIT AFFREUSE.LE BONHEUR SEMBLAIT ENFUI DANS TOUT CE QUI N'ÉTAIT PAS SON ILE.......
COSMAGE,DÉLAISSÉE,PLEURAIT.....

Edy Legrand
Macao et Cosmage, 1919

Edward Ardizzone
Little Tim and the Brave Sea Captain

ON THE TWELVTH DAY OF CHRIST-
MAS MY TRUE LOVE GAVE TO ME
TWELVE LADIES DANCING
LEVEN LORDS ALEAPING, TEN DRUM-
MERS DRUMMING, NINE PIPERS PIP-
ING, EIGHT MAIDS AMILKING, SEVEN
SWANS ASWIMMING, SIX GEESE A-
LAYING, FIVE GOLDEN RINGS, FOUR
COLLIE BIRDS, THREE FRENCH HENS,
TWO TURTLE DOVES AND A PARTRIDGE
IN A
PEAR
TREE

Ben Shahn
Double-spread from *A Partridge in a Pear Tree*

Ivan Chermayeff
Blind Mice and Other Numbers

Tony Palladino
The General

Paul Rand
Sparkle and Spin